Scott. Foresman and Company

School Songs by Grades

Fifth and Sixth Grades

Scott. Foresman and Company

School Songs by Grades
Fifth and Sixth Grades

ISBN/EAN: 9783744766807

Printed in Europe, USA, Canada, Australia, Japan

Cover: Foto ©Paul-Georg Meister /pixelio.de

More available books at **www.hansebooks.com**

HAYDN   MENDELSSOHN   SCHUBERT   MOZART

SCHOOL SONGS BY GRADES

UNISON SONGS, DUETS, CHORUSES
AND A FEW TRIOS

FOR

FIFTH AND SIXTH GRADES

———

CHICAGO
SCOTT, FORESMAN & COMPANY
1898

SONG SINGING.

SONG singing is so natural to childhood that if given merely for recreation or variety, children are liable to fall into the habit of regarding music not as a great and beautiful art, but as an amusement requiring neither effort nor earnest consideration; hence there may result a preference for catchy tunes and sprightly jingles. To cultivate in children a preference for the best—for what is essentially beautiful as against that which is merely striking—this is what song singing in the public schools should do, and what it can and will do if properly taught.

True Purpose of Song Singing.

The music hour in any school curriculum ought not, therefore, to be simply a time for recreation. Teachers who use it merely for adding variety to the programme, or as a period for relaxation, fail to understand the real purpose or true nature of music study. There should be no violent contrast between the methods of regular studies and the study of song singing. It is true, of course, that the time devoted to music should be restful, and that it should give both change and variety to the school programme; but these should result from the mastery of pleasing musical effects rather than from thoughtless singing. Every song presented to the child should be a good influence and a hidden discipline; it should also contain elements calculated to arouse in him a wholesome respect, which may finally develop into a love and reverence, for the divinity of song.

Use of Music Hour.

The Power of Song.

Again, the teacher should not cater to the pupil's love for novelty by constantly consulting the choice

Selection of Songs.

of the class, and yielding to the wishes of the majority. She herself should select the songs for the lesson, in order that a definite system may underlie all the work of the music hour. Desultory song singing, changing from one song to another, with no continuity of thought, gives the pupil an entirely wrong idea of the purpose of music in school work. The class should master whatever it undertakes. Gradual growth and a constant forward movement should result from every song effort. A definite purpose will inspire confidence, and the spirit of the pupil will respond to the spirit of the earnest teacher.

Value of Song Singing.

Songs have an educational value only when taught in an educational way. The intelligent mastery of the thought and feeling of a song is of far more value than the mere rendering of the tune.

School Songs by Grades

For Fifth and Sixth Grades.

In the Wood.

Marzano.

Wuerfel.

Allegro
mf

1. How love - ly is the wood, The green, the shad - y wood!
2. How we de - light to roam With - in our leaf - y home!
3. What pleas-ant sounds we hear Float down the wood so clear!

When mild-ly the breez - es are blowing, And free - ly our voic - es are
The branches are quiv - er - ing o'er us, And mur-mur their greetings be-
The ech - oes that ans - wer our sing-ing, From far the dim mes - sa - ges

flow - ing, Are flow - ing a - bout the wood, The
fore us All through the mist - y wood, The
bring - ing, From deeps with - in the wood, The

1st and 2nd verses.   3rd verse.

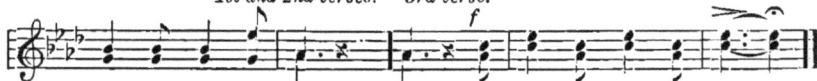

green, the shad - y wood.
green, the gold - en wood.
green, the hap - py wood. Hal - loo! hal - loo! hal - loo!

8

Now is the Month of Maying.

Vivace.
mf

German.

1. Now is the month of May - ing, La, la, la, la, la, la;
2. The spring, clad all in glad - ness, La, la, la, la, la, la;
3. Fie! then, why sit we mus - ing, La, la, la, la, la, la;

When mer - ry lads are play - ing, La, la, la, la, la, la;
Doth laugh at win - ter's sad - ness; La, la, la, la, la, la;
Youth's sweet de - lights re - fus - ing, La, la, la, la, la, la;

cresc.

And lass - es, too, are danc-ing, And steeds are gai - ly pranc-ing;
The mer - ry brook-let sound-ing, And ver - dure all a - bound-ing;
Be mer - ry in the time of spring, And let us gai - ly dance and sing;

f

Now is the month of May - ing. Now is the month of

p *cresc.* *f*

May - ing. La, la, la, la, la, la, la, la, la, la.

Praise in Song.

Andante.
mf

Naegeli.

1. Come, praise the Lord, He loves to hear you sing-ing. In sweet ac - cord
2. We're heard a - far In God's most ho-ly dwel-ling. So loud and clear
3. Our voic - es raise, With joy and gladness sing-ing; And cheer-ful praise

Loud let His praise be ring-ing; Come, praise the Lord; Oh! praise the Lord.
Our voic - es now are swell-ing; We're heard a - far, We're heard a - far.
Oh! let us all be bring-ing; Our voic - es raise, Our voic - es raise.

I.

II.

The Night is Past.

Kohl.

1. The night is past; We wake at last, For morn - ing now re-
2. In qui - et trust We sank to rest, In sleep fresh strength to

joic - es; To Thee a - bove, The God of love, We glad - ly
gath - er; Now glad - ly we Will work for Thee; Bless Thou our

raise our voic - es, We glad - ly raise our voic - es.
la - bor, Fa - ther, Bless Thou our la - bor, Fa - ther.

Sicilian Hymn.

Sicilian.

1. Heav'n-ly Fa - ther, grant Thy bless-ing On the teach-ing of this day;
2. Ev - 'ry mo - tive steadfast tend - ing, More and more to know and gain;

May we all, Thy love pos - sess-ing, Still pass on in wis-dom's way.
To a ho - ly pur - pose blending All the knowl-edge we at - tain.

10

The Spider and the Fly.

ROUND FOR THREE VOICES.

W. G. McNaught.

Allegretto.

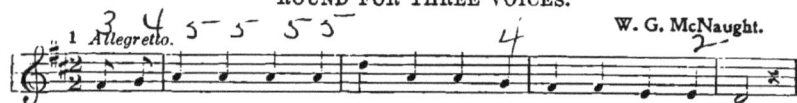

"Will you come in - to my par - lor?" said the spi - der to the fly,

"'Tis the pret - ti - est, snuggest lit - tle par - lor that ev - er you did' spy."

"Not to - day, thanks, Mis-ter Long-shanks, I've oth - er fish to fry."

Winter Time is Drawing Near.

Andante. Silcher.

1. Win - ter time is draw - ing near, And my heart is sink - ing;
2. Sum - mer birds have sung their last, From our cold land fly - ing;
3. Yes, we bid you all good - bye, Birds and bees and flow - ers;

Youth and life must dis - ap - pear, From the cold blast shrink-ing;
Sum - mer skies are o - ver - cast; Shril - ly winds are sigh - ing;
Sum - mer breez - es, sum - mer sky, Hap - py sum - mer hours;

cresc. *mf*

Woods must lose their leaf - y crown, Fields put on their coat of brown;
Not a but - ter - fly is seen, Hum - ming bee, nor bee - tle sheen;
Hear you not the au - tumn gale, Say - ing with its mourn - ful wail,

cresc. *rit.*

Ah! how sad is part - ing, Ah! how sad is part - ing.
Ah! how sad is part - ing, Ah! how sad is part - ing.
"Ah! how sad is part - ing, Sad, ah! sad is part - ing."

Copyright, 1897, by Scott, Foresman & Company.

Come Back, Sweet May.

11

Vivace. *mf*   cresc.   German.

1. Come back, come back, sweet May, And bid the flow-ers bloom, The birds sing on the
2.   I love the gold-en splen-dor Of gay and glo-rious June, I love the twi-light

spray, The skies their blue re - sume.   *mf*   Once more I would be breath-ing Thy
ten-der Of Au-tumn's har-vest-moon.   A - las! that all such hours   So

cresc.

fresh and fra-grant air, Once more I would be wreath-ing Thy blos-soms in my hair.
soon shall pass a-way.   Fill, fill thy lap with flow-ers; Come back, come back, sweet May.

p La la la la la la la la la la   *f* la la la la la la la la.

Suggestive Studies.

I.

II.

A Praise Song.

Montgomery.   Rinck.
Maestoso.

mf
1. Songs of praise the an-gels sang, Heav'n with hal - le - lu - jahs rang
2. Heav'n and earth must pass a - way, Songs of praise shall crown that day,
3. Here be - low, with heart and voice, We'll in songs of praise re - joice,

When Je - ho - vah's work be - gun, When He spoke, and it was done.
God will make new heav'ns and earth, Songs of praise shall hail their birth.
Learn-ing, thus by faith and love, Songs of praise to sing a - bove.

Oh! 'Twas Sweet to Hear Her.

Alexander Lee.

Moderato.

1. The ves - per bells were soft - ly, soft - ly ring - ing O'er the
2. And bright - est moon-beams tipt the moun - tain, While the

sil - ver'd, stil - ly lake; The night - in - gale was sweet-ly, sweetly
glow-worm crept a - long With lit - tle light near you cool

sing - ing Thro' the wood and tan - gled brake. Oh! 'twas sweet to
foun - tain, As she car - oll'd forth her song. Oh! 'twas sweet to

hear her sing-ing While the ves - per bells were ring-ing, Oh! 'twas sweet to
hear her sing-ing While the ves - per bells were ring-ing, Oh! 'twas sweet to

hear her sing - ing While the ves - per bells were ring - ing, Oh! 'twas
hear her sing - ing While the ves - per bells were ring - ing, Oh! 'twas

sweet to hear her, Oh! 'twas sweet to hear her sing - ing That
sweet to hear her, Oh! 'twas sweet to hear her sing - ing That

ser - aph, ser - aph song, To hear her sing-ing that sweet, sweet song.
ser - aph, ser - aph song, To hear her sing-ing that sweet, sweet song.

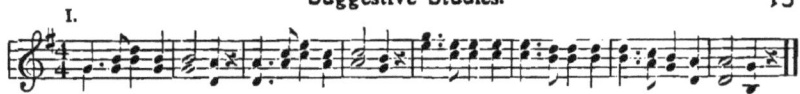

I.

II.

Drill Song.

Andante.

Folk Song.

mf

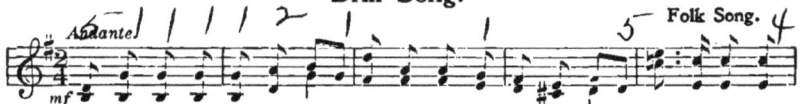

1. Let us have a drill to - day, March a-long in grand ar - ray; And who - ever
2. Stepping all in time we go, Sol-diers marching in a row; As we gai-ly
3. Active feet and ready rhyme, Steps and voices well must chime; Left foot, right foot,
4. In two ranks let us di - vide, March a-long on eith-er side; And soon marching

steps the best Shall be cap-tain o'er the rest, Lead us on our way.
move a - long, Sing-ing still our march-ing song, Marching to and fro.
for - ward, all. March on, children, great and small, March a-way in time.
as be - fore, Each his part-ner has once more: Then our drill is o'er.

Gently Evening Bendeth.

Andantino, dolce

Fesca.

p

1. Gen-tly ev'n-ing bend-eth O - ver vale and hill, O - ver vale and hill;
2. Save the wood-brook's gushing, All things silent rest, All things silent rest;
3. Rest-less thus life flow-eth, Striv-eth in my breast, Striv-eth in my breast;

dim.   pp

Soft-ly peace de-scend-eth, And the world is still, And the world is still.
Hear it rest-less rush-ing On tow'rds o-cean's breast, On tow'rds o-cean's breast.
God a-lone be-stow - eth Tranquil even-ing rest, Tran-quil even-ing rest.

I.

II.

Spinning Song.

Kreuz.
Andante.

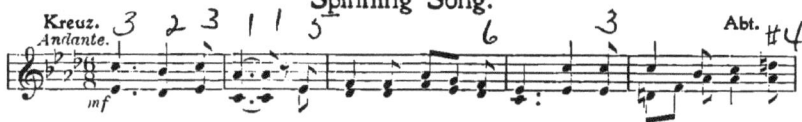

1.   Spin, las - sie, spin; The thread goes out and in; Growing like your yellow
2.   Sing, las - sie, sing;   A mer - ry heart to bring; As your spin-ning you be-
3.   Learn, las - sie, learn, Your dai - ly bread to earn; Learn to work, and learn to

hair, Sense will grow from year to year: Spin, las-sie, spin;   Spin, las-sie, spin.
gin; Keep a cheerful heart with-in: Sing, las-sie, sing;   Sing, las-sie, sing.
pray, Spinning on from day to day: Learn, las-sie, learn;   Learn, las-sie, learn.

Hunting Song.

Paul Whitehead.   Andre.
Allegretto. Dolce

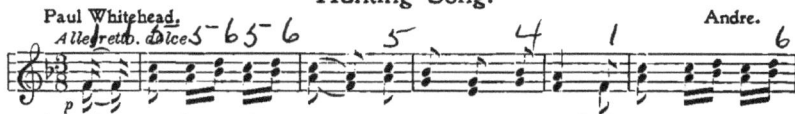

1.   The sun from the   east tips the mountains with gold; The mead-ows all
2. Let the drudge of the   town make rich - es his sport, The slave of   the

span-gled with dew-drops be-hold. Hear! the lark's ear - ly   mat - in pro-
state hunt the smiles of   a court,—No   care and am -   bi - tion our
                     CHO.—With the sports of   the   field there's no

claims the new   day, And the horn's cheer-ful   summons rebukes our de - lay.
pastime an - noy, But   in - no - cence   still gives a   zest to our joy.
pleas-ure can   vie, While   joc - und we   fol - low the hounds in full cry.

Come, May, in All Thy Beauty.

Overbeck.

Allegretto. dolce

Mozart.

p

1. Come, May, in all thy beau - ty, And deck the groves a - gain,
2. True, win - ter days have ma - ny And ma - ny a dear de - light;
3. But, oh! when comes the sea - son For mer - ry birds to sing,

And let thy silv - 'ry stream-lets Me - an - der thro' the plain;
We frol - ic in the snow-drifts, And then the win - ter - night
How sweet to roam in mead - ows, And drink the breeze of spring!

We long once more to gath - er The flow'r - ets fresh and fair,
A - round the fire we clust - er, Nor heed the whist - ling storm;
Then, come, sweet May, and bring us The flow'r - et fresh and fair;

Sweet May, once more to wan - der, And breathe the balm - y air.
When all with - out is drea - ry Our hearts are bright and warm.
We long once more to wan - der, And breathe thy balm - y air.

Yesterday.

Andante.

German.

mf

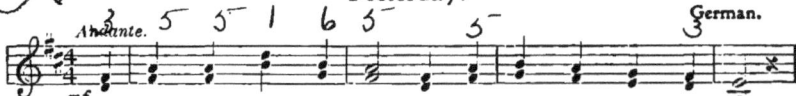

1. But yes - ter - day the gar - den Was gay with bright-est hues;
2. To - day, they all are fad - ed, Their beau - ty all is fled,
3. But soon the spring re - turn - ing Up - on her ros - y car,

cresc. *dim.*

The flow'rs, all fresh and love - ly, And bright with morn - ing dews,
Their frag - ile forms are brok - en, Thin, with-ered now, and dead,
Will bring the word com-mand-ing The buds to burst once more,

cresc. *dim.*

The flow'rs, all fresh and love - ly, And bright with morn-ing dews.
Their frag - ile forms are brok - en, Thin, with-ered now, and dead.
Will bring the word com-mand - ing The buds to burst once more.

16

The Hunter's Song.

Joanna Baillie. *Con spirito.*

Albert Voelckerling.

mf

Con spirito.

mf

1. The chough and crow to roost have gone, The owl sits on a tree, The
2. Nor board nor gar - ner own we now, Nor roof nor latch - ed door, Nor

hushed wind wails with fee - ble moan Like in - fant char - i - ty, The
kind mate, bound by ho - ly vow To bless a good man's store; Noon

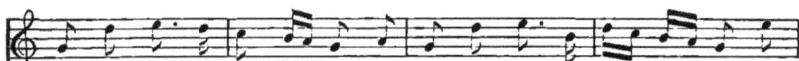

wild fire danc - es on the fen, The red star sheds its ray, its ray; Up-
lulls us in a gloom - y den, And night has grown our day, our day; Up-

rouse ye, then, my mer - ry men, Up-rouse ye, then, my mer - ry men, It
rouse ye, then, my mer - ry men, Up-rouse ye, then, my mer - ry men, It

The Hunter's Song.

is　our　op-'ning　day,　It　　is　　our　　op - 'ning, op - 'ning　day,　　Up-
is　our　op-'ning　day,　It　　is　　our　　op - 'ning, op - 'ning　day,　　Up-

rouse,　　　up-rouse,　　　It　　is　　our　op - 'ning　day.
rouse,　　　up-rouse,　　　It　　is　　our　op - 'ning　day.

m. s.　　　　　*m. s.*

Hark! the Bell's Ding, Dong.

ROUND.

Andante.　　　　　　　　　　　　　　　　　　　　　　*Silcher.*

mf

Hark! the bell's ding, dong　Calls us　to　our　song,　Calls us　to　our

song,......　to　our song　Hark! the bell's ding, dong　Calls us　to　our

song,　Calls　us　to　our　song,........　to　our　song.

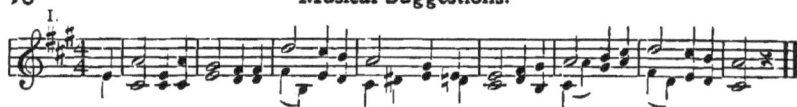

I.

II.

Winter.

Whittier.   Allegro.   Methfessel.

mf

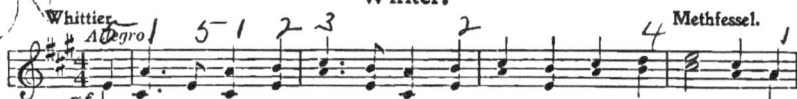

1. Old win - ter is a sturd - y one, And last - ing stuff he's made of; His
2. He spreads his coat up - on the heath, Nor yet, to warm it, lin - gers; He
3. His home is by the North Pole's strand, Where earth and sea are froz - en; His

flesh is hard as i - ron-stone; There's nothing he's a - fraid of.
scouts the thought of ach - ing teeth Or chil-blains on his fin - gers.
sum-mer house, we un - der-stand, In Switz - er - land he's chos - en.

Day - Break.

Allegretto.   Methfessel.   *cresc.*

mf

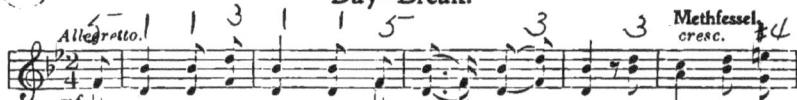

1. See, day-light is com - ing with all her gay train, To earth bring-ing
2. The wild birds now car - ol their sweet morn-ing-song, And hill-side and
3. While all else re - joic - es, shall man si - lent be? No! we'll join the

dim.

beau - ty and bright-ness a - gain; Night's shad-ows are flee - ing now
moun-tain the ech - oes pro-long; The riv - u - let mur-murs a
cho - rus with earth and with sea; And praise Him who gave us the

cresc.   *dim.*

swift-ly a - way, While light is pro - claim-ing the her-ald of day.
mel - o - dy sweet, Which earth and the o - cean in cho-rus re-peat.
morn bright and gay, And ask His pro - tec - tion thro'out the glad day.

All Things Well.

John Keble.   Naegeli.

1. All things bright and beau-ti-ful, All creat-ures great and small,
2. The pur - ple-head - ed moun-tain, The riv - er run-ning by,
3. The tall trees in the green-wood, The mead-ows where we play,

All things wise and won-der-ful,— The Lord God made them all.
The sun - set and the morn - ing That bright-en up the sky,
The rush - es by the wa - ter We gath-er ev - 'ry day,

Each lit - tle flow'r that o - pens, Each lit - tle bird that sings,
The cold wind and the win - ter, The pleas - ant sum-mer sun,
He gave us eyes, to see them, And lips, that we might tell

He made their glow - ing col - ors, He made their shin-ing wings.
The ripe fruit in the gar - den,— He made them ev - 'ry one.
How great is God Al - might - y, Who do - eth all things well.

Sunset Breeze.

Murray.   German.
Moderate

1. Soft - ly sighs the sunset breeze; Vesper bells are ring - ing; O'er the earth on
2. Gen-tly fades the ev - 'ning red; Vesper chimes are dy - ing; Nature thrills with
3. Fainter beat my puls-es all; Dreamy vis - ions haunt me; Would that from this

bend-ed knees, O'er the earth on bend-ed knees, Night her veil is fling-ing.
ho - ly dread, Na - ture thrills with ho - ly dread, Hush'd is e'en her sigh-ing.
bless-ed thrall, Would that from this blessed thrall Naught could dis-en-chant me!

If We Knew.

Cary.
Moderato

German.

mf

1. Strange we nev - er prize the mu - sic Till the sweet-voiced bird has flown;
2. Let us gath-er up the sunbeams, Ly-ing all a - bout our path;

Strange that we should slight the vio - lets Till the love-ly flowers are gone;
Let us keep the wheat and ros - es, Casting out the thorns and chaff;

Strange that summer skies and sunshine Nev-er seem one - half so fair
Let us find our sweet-est com-fort In the bless-ings of to - day,

As when winter's snow-y pin-ions Shake their white down in the air.
With a pa-tient hand re - mov-ing All the bri - ars from the way.

Praise Song.

Milton.
Moderato

Silcher.

cresc.

mf

1. Let us with a joy - ful mind Praise the Lord, for
2. Let us sound His name a - broad, For of all He
3. All His crea - tures God doth feed, His full hand sup -
4. He His man - sion hath on high, 'Bove the reach of

He is kind; For His mer - cies shall en - dure, Ev - er faith - ful,
is the God Who by wis - dom did cre - ate Heav'n a - bove in
plies their need; Let us, there-fore, war - ble forth His high maj - es -
mor - tal eye; And His mer-cies shall en - dure, Ev - er faith - ful,

f Ev - er faith - ful, ev - er sure.

ev er sure, Ev - er faith - ful, ev - er sure.
all its state, Heav'n a - bove in all its state.
ty and worth, His high maj - es - ty and worth.
ev - er sure, Ev - er faith - ful, ev - er sure.

All The Birds Have Come Again.

Hoffmann von Fallersleben.   German.

Allegretto

mf

1. All the birds have come a - gain, Come a - gain, to meet us;
2. See, how gai - ly one and all To and fro are spring - ing!
3. What they teach us in their song, We must e'er be learn - ing;

p

And a joy - ous song they raise, Chirp - ing, trill - ing mer - ry lays;
As their chant - ing meets my ear Voic - es sweet I seem to hear,
Let us ev - er cheer - ful be As the birds up - on the tree,

mf

Pleas - ant spring - time's hap - py days Now re - turn to greet us.
Wish - ing me a hap - py year, Bless - ings with it bring - ing.
Wel - com - ing so joy - ous - ly Ev - 'ry spring re - turn - ing.

Awake! Awake! The Dawn Is Here.

Oxenford.   A. S. Gatty.

Solo. Allegro.   CHORUS.

mf

1. A - wake! a - wake! the dawn is here, Ring, morn - ing bells, ding, dong!
2. On ev - 'ry hill, in dale and dell, Ring, morn - ing bells, ding, dong!
3. The birds with - in the shad - y wood, Ring, morn - ing bells, ding, dong!

SOLO.   CHORUS.

Shrill crows the warn - ing chan - ti - cleer, Ring, morn - ing bells, ding, dong!
The flow'rs o - bey the po - tent spell, Ring, morn - ing bells, ding, dong!
Chant mat - ins to their ti - ny brood, Ring, morn - ing bells, ding, dong!

SOLO.   *rall.*

The sun, ar - rayed in gold and red, Is ris - ing from his east - ern bed.
And ope their sleep - ing cup a - new, A wel - come to the in - fant dew.
And trill with joy a dul - cet lay, A wel - come to the in - fant day.

CHORUS. *a tempo*   *cresc.*   *f*

mf

Ring, morn - ing bells, Ring, morn - ing bells, Ring, morning bells, ding, dong!

The Brook.

Tennyson.
Allegretto.

Zelter.

p

1. I come from haunts of coot and hern, I make a sud - den sal - ly,
2. I steal by lawns and grass - y plots, I slide by ha - zel cov - ers;
3. I mur - mur un - der moon and stars, In balm - y wil - der - ness - es;

And spar-kle out a - mong the fern, To bick - er down a val - ley.
I move the sweet for - get - me - nots That grow for hap - py lov - ers.
I lin - ger by my shing - ly bars, I loi - ter round my cress - es;

By thir - ty hills I hur - ry down, Or slip be - tween the
I slip, I slide, I gloom, I glance, A - mong the skim - ming
And out a - gain I curve and flow, To join the brim - ming

cresc.   *mf*

ridg - es, Or slip be - tween the ridg - es, By
swal - lows, A - mong the skim - ming swal - lows; I
riv - er, To join the brim - ming riv - er; For

twen - ty thorps, a lit - tle town, And half a hun - dred bridg-es.
make the net - ted sun-beam dance A - gainst my sand - y shal-lows.
men may come and men may go, But I go on for - ev - er.

A Maple Leaf.

James Geddes.
Moderato.

W. Volkmann.

p

mf

1. A ma - ple leaf, whose gown was red, Glanced gai-ly at her fel - low,
2. "Oh! what a night to dance the lea," She said in ac - cents spright-ly,
3. The au-tumn breez - es piped a jig, The brook-let hummed a dit - ty,
4. I heard, de - part - ing down the glen, Their trip-ping steps and laugh-ter;

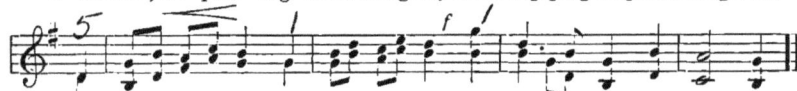

f

A birch - en leaf with or - ange cap And doublet trimmed with yel - low.
He straight-way doffed his silk - en cap, In - vit - ing her po - lite - ly.
As swift and swift - er flew their feet, They grew more gay and wit - ty.
But where they went, I do not know; I did not fol - low aft - er.

1. Come, gen-tle May, we pray thee, And make the mead-ows
2. Come, send the ten-der show-ers That wake the germs be-

green, In blos-soms white ar-ray thee, Let vio-lets
low. Then o-pen buds and flow-ers, Then rud-dy

too be seen. Oh! deck the hedg-es yon-der With hawthorn,
ros-es blow. For these sweet joys we ask thee, we ask thee,

May Song.

with haw - thorn and with May,   The
O boun - teous, smil - ing May!   In

chil - dren forth would wan-der, would wan - der forth, And thro' the
clouds no lon - ger mask thee, Oh! come,........ oh! come, and let the

wood - land stray!
earth be gay!

Jack Frost.

Elizabeth B. Beebee.

German.

Allegro. marcato

cresc.

mf

1. Old Jack Frost has come to town, boys, Win-ter's dear-est, chos-en friend;
2. Such a qui-et wir-y fel-low, But his han-di-work is seen
3. He will nip your toes and fin-gers, But he'll help to draw your sled;

He will sport up-on the breez-es, And a sea-son with us spend.
In the pic-tures on the glass-pane, And the wa-ter's crys-tal sheen.
And he'll set your blood a-ting-ling, Till your cheeks are ros-y red.

f

La la la la la, la la la la la, La, la la la la, la la la la la.

Brother Robin.

Mrs. Anderson.

Seidel.

Allegretto

mf

1. Lis-ten! with the A-pril rain Broth-er Rob-in's here a-gain;
2. He has neith-er grief nor care; Build-ing sites are ev-'ry-where;

Songs like show-ers come and go; Rob-in's build-ing house, I know.
If one nest is blown a-way, Fields are full of sticks and hay.

Tho' he finds, the old pine tree Is not where it used to be,
Tho' old mous-ing puss last year Ate his lit-tle ones, I fear,

And the nest he made last year, Torn and scat-tered far and near.
And he al-most died of fright, That is all for-got-ten quite.

The Star-Spangled Banner.

Key:
Maestoso.

1. Oh! say, can you see, by the dawn's ear - ly light, What so
2. On the shore, dim - ly seen thro' the mist of the deep, Where the
3. And where is that band who so vaunt - ing - ly swore That the
4. Oh! thus be it e'er when free - men shall stand Be -

proud - ly we hail'd at the twi - light's last gleam - ing, Whose
foe's haught-y host in dread si - lence re - pos - es, What is
hav - oc of war and the bat - tle's con - fu - sion, A
tween their lov'd homes and the war's des - o - la - tion; Blest with

broad stripes and stars thro' the per - il - ous fight, O'er the ram - parts we
that which the breeze, o'er the tow - er - ing steep As it fit - ful - ly
home and a coun - try shall leave us no more? Their blood has washed
vict' - ry and peace, may the heav'n-res-cued land Praise the pow'r that hath

watch'd were so gal - lant - ly stream-ing? And the rock-ets' red glare, the bombs
blows, half con-ceals, half dis - clos - es? Now it catch-es the gleam of the
out their foul foot-step's pol - lu - tion; No ref - uge can save the
made and pre-serv'd us a na - tion; Then, con - quer we must when our

burst - ing in air, Gave proof thro' the night that our
morn - ing's first beam, In full glo - ry re - flec - ted, now
hire - ling and slave From the ter - ror of flight or the
cause it is just, And this be our mot - to, "In

cresc.

flag was still there; Oh! say, does the star-span-gled ban - ner still
shines on the stream; 'Tis the star-span - gled ban-ner, oh! long may it
gloom of the grave. And the star-span - gled ban-ner in tri - umph shall
God is our trust." And the star-span - gled ban-ner in tri - umph shall

ff

rit.

wave O'er the land of the free and the home of the brave?

Birds are Singing.

Hoffmann von Fallersleben.

Fesca.

Allegretto.

1. Birds are sing - ing, flow'rs are spring-ing, Green are fields and woods once
2. Birds are sit - ting in their bow - ers, We of late have sat at
3. Joy is burst - ing forth a - round us, O'er the hills, a - cross the
4. Let us, then, go forth and wan - der By the stream-let, thro' the

mf

more; We will go and seek earth's treas - ures, We will
home; Gone is gloom - y win - ter's sad - ness, We can
vales; Far and wide by breez - es draft - ed, On the
lane, By the hedge - row flow - er - stud - ded, By the

taste our new - sent pleas -ures, Wand'ring o'er earth's grass - y floor.
now go forth in glad - ness, Ev - 'ry-where we now may roam.
scent - ed flow - ers waft - ed, And the songs of night - in - gales.
trees which now have bud - ded, Thro' the new - born world a - gain.

Over the Summer Sea.

Andante.

Verdi.

mf

1. O - ver the sum - mer sea, With light hearts gay and free, Joined by glad
2. List! there's a bird on high, Far in yon a - zure sky, Fling-ing sweet

min-strel-sy, Gai - ly we're roam-ing; Swift flows the rippling tide; Lightly the
mel - o - dy, Each heart to glad-den; Hark! its song seems to say, Ban-ish dull

zephyrs glide; Round us, on ev'ry side, Bright crests are foaming; Fond hearts en-
care a - way, Nev-er let sor-row stay, Bright joys to sad-den; Fond hearts en-

cresc.

f

twin-ing, Cease all re - pin-ing; Near us is shin-ing Beauty's bright smile.
twin-ing, Cease all re - pin-ing; Near us is shin-ing Beauty's bright smile.

The Marseillaise Hymn.

Rouget de l'Isle?

Allegro.

1. Ye sons of free-dom, wake to glo - ry, Hark! hark! what myriads bid you
2. Now, now the dang'rous storm is roll-ing Which treach'rous kings confederate
3. O Lib - er - ty, can man re - sign thee, Once hav-ing felt thy gen'rous

rise. Your chil - dren, wives, and grand - sires hoar - y, Be - hold their
raise; The dogs of war, let loose, are howl - ing, And lo! our
flame? Can dun-geons, bolts, or bars con - fine thee? Or whips thy

tears and hear their cries, Be-hold their tears and hear their cries; Shall hateful
fields and cit - ies blaze, And lo! our fields and cit - ies blaze; And shall we
no - ble spir - it tame? Or whips thy no - ble spir - it tame? Too long the

ty-rants, mis-chiefs breeding, With hireling hosts, a ruf - fian band, Af-
base - ly view the ru - in While lawless force with guilt - y stride Spreads
world has wept, be - wail - ing That falsehood's dagger ty - rants wield; But

fright and des - o - late the land, While peace and lib - er - ty lie bleed-ing?
des - o - la - tion far and wide, With crimes and blood his hands imbruing?
free - dom is our sword and shield, And all their arts are un - a - vail - ing.

REFRAIN.

To arms! to arms! ye brave, Th'a - veng - ing sword un-sheathe;

March on, march on, all hearts re-solved On vic - to - ry or death.

The Skylark.

J. Hogg.
Andante.

A. R. Gaul.
cresc.

mf
1. Bird of the wil - der - ness, Blithesome and cum - ber - less, Sweet be thy
2. O'er fell and foun-tain sheen, O'er moor and mountain green, O'er the red

dim.

mat - in o'er moor-land and lea! Em - blem of hap - pi - ness,
stream - er that her - alds the day, O - ver the cloud - let dim,

Blest is thy dwell - ing-place. Oh! to a - bide in the des - ert with
O - ver the rain - bow's rim, Mu - si - cal cher - ub, soar, sing-ing, a-

mf
thee. Wild is thy lay and loud Far in the down - y cloud,
way. Then, when the gloam-ing comes Low in the heath - er blooms,

cresc.   dim.

Love gives it en - er - gy, love gave it birth. Where, on thy
Sweet will thy wel - come and bed of love be. Em - blem of

mf   f
dew - y wing, Where art thou jour - ney - ing? Thy lay in heav-en, thy
hap - pi - ness, Blest is thy dwell - ing-place. Oh! to a - bide in the

mf
love... on earth. } Bird of the wil - der - ness, Blithesome and
des - ert with thee. }

rall.

cum - ber - less, Oh! to a - bide in the des - ert with thee.

Violet, My Violet!

Moderato
p dolce

Staab.
cresc.

1. Vi - o - let, my vi - o - let, In my gar-den grow-ing, Why look'st thou so
2. Vi - o - let, my vi - o - let, In - no-cent thy face is. Dost thou hide the

mf

p più lento

know-ing, In my gar-den grow-ing, In my gar - den grow-ing?
Gra - ces Un - der-neath thy fa - ces, Un - der - neath thy fa - ces?

O Summer Morning!

E. Fitzball.
Allegretto.

C. A. Kern.

mf

1. O Sum - mer morn-ing fresh and bright, When in the hedge wild
2. When skies look blue and birds sing sweet, And dew-drops glit - ter

ros - es blow, And per - fumed breez - es pure and light Scarce
on the thorn, And dai - sied car - pets tempt the feet,— Oh!

wave the green boughs to and fro, Scarce wave the green boughs to and fro.
love - ly, love-ly then art thou, Oh! love-ly, love - ly then art thou.

Before All Lands in East or West.

Allegro moderato.

mf

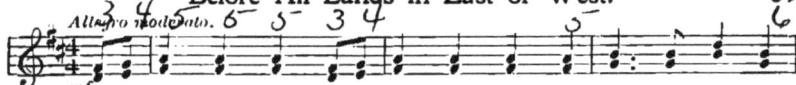

1. Be - fore all lands in east or west, I love my na - tive
2. Be - fore all tongues in east or west, I love my na - tive
3. Be - fore all peo - ple, east or west, I love my coun-try-
4. To all the world I give my hand, My heart I give my

land the best, With God's best gifts 'tis teem - ing; For gold and jew - els
tongue the best; Tho' not so smooth-ly spok - en, Nor wov - en with I-
men the best, A race of no - ble spir - it; A so - ber mind, a
na - tive land; I seek her good, her glo - ry; I hon - or ev - 'ry

here are found, And men of no - ble worth a - bound, And
tal - ian art; Yet, when it speaks from heart to heart, The
gen - 'rous heart, To vir - tue trained, yet free from art, They
na - tion's name, Re - spect their for - tune and their fame; But

eyes of joy are beam - ing, And eyes of joy are beam - ing.
word is nev - er bro - ken, The word is nev - er bro - ken.
from their sires in - her - it, They from their sires in - her - it.
love the land that bore me, But love the land that bore me.

A. J. Foxwell.

Land of Greatness.

Haydn.

Moderato

mf

1. Land of great-ness, home of glo - ry, Land and birth-place of the free,
2. No - ble deeds of old in - spir - ing Ev - 'ry heart with loft - y aim,

Famed a - like in song and sto - ry, All thy sons shall cleave to thee.
Now our em - u - la - tion fir - ing, Lead us on to great - er fame.

cresc.

North and South are firm - ly band-ed, East and West as one u - nite,
So shall Free-dom's cause un-shak - en, No - ble cour - age, high - est worth,

dim.

All by hon - or well com-mand-ed, Strong in striv - ing for the right.
Might-y ech - oes still a - wak - en To the farth - est bounds of earth.

32

Suggestive Study.

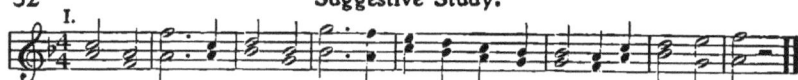

I.

II.

When the Stars.

English.

Allegretto.

mf

1. When the stars, at set of sun, Watch you from on high; When the morn-ing
2. All you do, and all you say, He can see and hear; When you work, and
3. All your joys and griefs He knows, Counts each falling tear; When to Him you
4. What we do as in His sight, We can do with ease; Ev-'ry task be-

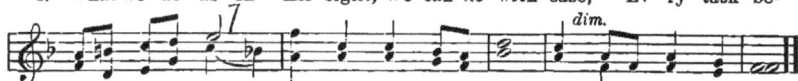

dim.

is	be-	gun;	Think the Lord	is	nigh, Think the	Lord	is nigh.
when	you	play	Think the Lord	is	near, Think the	Lord	is near.
tell	your	woes	Think the Lord	will hear, Think the	Lord	will hear.
comes	more	light	When we think	He	sees, When	we	think He sees.

Winter Flowers.

Allegro moderato.

Alfred Moffat.

1. Now the winds of win-ter blow Fierce-ly thro' the chil-ly air;
2. Noth-ing but the hol-ly bright, Spot-ted with its ber-ries gay;
3. Or the hip of shin-ing red Where the wild-rose used to blow,

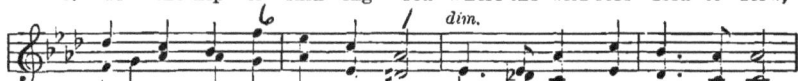

dim.

Now the fields are white with snow, Can we find a po-sy there?
Laur-is-tin-us, red and white; Or the i-vy's crook-ed spray
Peep-ing out its scar-let head From be-neath a cap of snow;

mf   cresc.   f

No, there can-not all a-round Sin-gle blade of grass be found.
With a sloe of dark-some blue Where the rag-ged black-thorn grew.
These are all that dare to stay Through this chil-ly win-ter's day.

Copyright, 1897, by Scott, Foresman & Company.

Home, Sweet Home!

Payne.   Irish.

Moderato. dolce. cresc.   dim.

1. 'Mid pleas-ures and pal - a - ces though we may roam, Be it
2. An ex - ile from home, splen - dor daz - zles in vain; Oh!
3. How sweet 'tis to sit 'neath a fond fa - ther's smile, And the
4. To thee I'll re - turn, o - ver - bur-den'd with care; The

cresc.   dim.   dim.

ev - er so hum-ble, there's no place like home. A charm from the skies seems to
give me my low - ly, thatch'd cottage a-gain; The birds singing gai - ly, that
cares of a moth - er to soothe and be-guile! Let oth - ers de - light 'mid new
heart's dearest sol - ace will smile on me there; No more from that cot-tage a-

dim.

f   mf

hal - low us there, Which, seek thro' the world, is ne'er met with else-where;
come at my call, Give me them with the peace of mind, dear - er than all.
pleasures to roam, But give me, oh! give me the pleas-ures of home.
gain will I roam,—Be it ev - er so hum - ble, there's no place like home.

cresc.   mf   dim.

p   mf   p
Home, home, sweet, sweet home! There's no place like home, There's no place like home.

The Traveler's Return.

Robert Southey   C. A. Kern.

8va   cresc.   dim.

mf

1. Sweet to the morn-ing trav - el - er The song a - mid the sky
2. And cheer-ing to the trav - el - er The gales that 'round him play
3. But, oh! of all de - light-ful sounds Of ev - 'ning or of morn,

dim.

Where, twinkling in the dew - y light, The sky - lark soars on high.
When faint and heav - i - ly he drags A - long his noon-tide way.
The sweet-est is the voice of love That wel-comes his re - turn.

Fairies' Song.

Oxenford.

Allegretto.

Albert Voelckerling.

1. A - round and round the
2. A - mid the flow'rs we

ma-gic ring We fair-ies laugh, and dance, and sing, And high in air for
sport and play, Like light-ning leap from spray to spray, And toss the dew-drops

glad - ness spring With swift and nim-ble feet. La la la, la la la,
far a - way A-mong the ferns and grass. La la la, la la la,

la la la la, la la, la la la, la la la, la la la, la, la la!

When the Boats Come Home.

T. Moore.
Andante
mf

W. Volkmann.

1. There's light up - on the sea to - day And glad-ness on the
2. We tend the chil - dren, live our life, And toil, and mend the
3. There's glo - ry on the sea to - day, The sun - set gold is

strand; Ah! well ye know that hearts are gay When
nets; But is there ev - er maid or wife Whose
bright; Methought I heard a grand - sire say, "At

sails draw nigh the land. We fol-lowed them with thoughts and tears Far,
faith - ful heart for-gets? We know what cru - el dan - gers lie Be-
eve it shall be light." O'er waves of crys - tal, touched with fire, And

far a - cross the foam; Dear Lord, it seems a
neath that shin - ing foam, And watch the chang - es
flakes of pear - ly foam, We gaze, and see our

thou-sand years Un - til the boats come home, Un - til the boats come home.
in the sky Un - til the boats come home, Un - til the boats come home.
hearts' de-sire, The boats are com - ing home, The boats are com - ing home.

36 The Noontide Ray.

Allegretto.   Arranged from Auber.

1. The mid - day sun is pour - ing His scorch - ing beams a -
2. The herds in shade are pant - ing, The leaves hang droop - ing
3. The wa - ters bright are shin - ing, Re - flect - ing back the

long the sky, No more the birds are soar - - ing, The
on the bough; No more her sweet song chant - ing, The
noon - tide ray; The vales and hills seem pin - - ing Be -

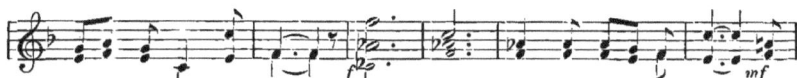

flow'-rets droop and die. Fly, then, sis - ter spir - its, fly; The
thrush is si - lent now. Hide, then, sis - ter spir - its, hide; The
neath the burn-ing day. Rest, then, sis - ter spir - its, rest; The

mid - day sun is pour - ing His beams a - long the sky.
herds in shade are pant - ing, The leaves droop on the bough.
wa - ters bright are shin - ing Be - neath the noon - tide ray.

In the West the Sun Declining.

Moderato.   cresc.   dim.   Abt.

1. In the west the sun de - clin - ing Sinks be-neath the moun-tain height,
2. Bleak - er winds the flow'rs be-numb-ing, On the hearth the crick - et sings;
3. Man now seeks his peace - ful dwell-ing, Cir - cles round the rud - dy blaze,

Tints the clouds with gold-en lin - ing, Sets the hills with ru - bies shin-ing,
Home the la - den bee flies hum-ming; And the drow - sy bat is com-ing,
Of the sweets of la - bor tell - ing Till his heart, with rap - ture swell-ing,

Then bids all the world good-night. Good night, good night, good night, good night!
Dart - ing on his leath - ern wings. Good night, good night, good night, good night!
Grate-ful gives his Mak - er praise. Good night, good night, good night, good night!

Now Good Night.

Naegeli.

Adagio.

mf

1. Now, good night! now, good night! Thus the wea - ry we in - vite.
2. Seek re - pose, seek re - pose, Let the wea - ry eye - lids close.
3. Now, good night! now, good night! Sleep till day-spring wakes on high,

mf

cresc.

p

Wan - ing day in si - lence flows, And all bu - sy hands re -
Si - lence reign-eth in the streets, With his horn the watch - man
Fear - less-ly un - til the day Strews new cares up - on thy

p

cresc.

pose... Till the dark - ness wakes.. to light.....
greets, And the night sighs as.... it flows.....
way.. Watch - ful is the Fa - - ther's eye!......

cresc.

p   *pp*

Now, good night! now, good night! now,...... good night!
Seek re - pose, seek re - pose, seek...... re - pose.
Now, good night! now, good night! now,...... good night!

p   *pp*

God's Providence.

Hey.

Andantino dolce

German.

1. Canst thou count the stars that twin-kle As they lie in God's dear hand?
2. Canst thou count the in-sects dan-cing In the joy-ous sum-mer sun?
3. Canst thou count the gay, young fa-ces That each morn-ing's rays a-wake,

Canst thou count the clouds that sprin-kle Rain-drops on the thirst-y land?
Canst thou count the swal-lows glan-cing Past us on their air-y run?
All who their ac-cus-tomed pla-ces In the round of life re-take?

God, the Lord, He knows their reck'ning, None, but must o-bey His beck'ning,
God, He call'd them in-to be-ing, None is born without His see-ing,
God, He knows them, ev-'ry one; None is left by Him a-lone,

cresc.

Of the shin-ing myr-iad host, Of the shin-ing my-riad host.
Where they are, and what they need, Where they are, and what they need.
Each He knows, and each He loves, Each He knows, and each He loves.

Joyfulness Is the Spice of Life.

Vivace.

ROUND.

Schneider.

cresc. *dim.*

mf

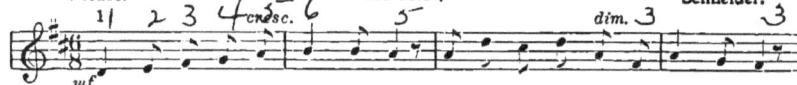

Joy-ful-ness is the spice of life, Let, therefore, sadness be cast a-side.

2 *cresc.* *dim.*

Joy-ful-ness is the spice of life, Let, therefore, sadness be cast a-side.

3 *cresc.* *dim.*

Joy-ful-ness is the spice of life, Let, therefore, sadness be cast a-side.

I.

II.

My Native Land.

Andante

Wohlfahrt.

mf
1. Faith-ful lov - ing,   no-bly prov-ing,   This I swear with heart and hand, All I
2. Brings to-mor-row   joy or sor - row, Still, my heart will constant be; Coun-try

Andante.

mf

am,   and all   I   may be,   It is thine, my fa - ther-land. Not a-
mine, with bonds e - ter - nal   All thy sons   are knit to thee. Faith-ful

My Native Land.

lone in tune-ful meas-ure Will I praise thee while I live; For thy
lov-ing, no-bly prov-ing, This I swear with heart and hand, All I

free-dom,dear-est treas-ure,Glad-ly I my life would give.
am, and all I may be, It is thine,my fa-ther-land.

Song of the Daisy.

Allegretto. *p*

Kern.

1. I'd rath-er be a dai-sy, The lit-tle chil-dren's flower, Than
2. When song and shout and laugh-ter Are ech-oed o'er the lea, Oh!
3. Come forth from crowd-ed ci-ties, From cas-tle and from hall, From
4. The sun hath dried the dew-drops, The grass is green and long, All

an - y proud-er beau-ty That decks my la-dy's bower.
mer-ry is the mu-sic Of child-hood's voice to me.
play-ground and from school-room, And I will greet you all.
o - ver starred with flow-ers That on-ly ask your song.

Columbia, the Gem of the Ocean;
or, The Red, White, and Blue.

David T. Shaw.
Maestoso.

D. T. S.

1. O Co-lum-bia! the gem of the o-cean, The home of the
2. When war winged its wide des-o-la-tion, And threatened the
3. The Un-ion, the Un-ion for-ev-er, Our glo-ri-ous

brave and the free, The shrine of each pa-triot's de-vo-tion, A
land to de-form, The ark then of free-dom's foun-da-tion, Co-
na-tion's sweet hymn, May the wreaths it has won nev-er with-er, Nor the

world of-fers hom-age to thee; Thy man-dates make he-roes as-
lum-bia rode safe thro' the storm, With her gar-lands of vic-t'ry a-
star of its glo-ry grow dim! May the ser-vice u-nit-ed ne'er

sem-ble When Lib-er-ty's form stands in view; Thy ban-ners make
round her, When so proudly she bore her brave crew, With her flag proudly
sev-er, But they to their col-ors prove true! The Ar-my and

tyr-an-ny trem-ble, When borne by the red, white, and blue.
float-ing be-fore her, The boast of the red, white, and blue.
Na-vy for-ev-er, Three cheers for the red, white, and blue.

CHORUS.

When borne by the red, white, and blue, When borne by the red, white, and blue, Thy
The boast of the red, white, and blue, The boast of the red, white, and blue, With her
Three cheers for the red, white, and blue, Three cheers for the red, white, and blue, The

ban-ners make tyr-an-ny tremble, When borne by the red, white, and blue.
flag proud-ly float-ing be-fore her, The boast of the red, white, and blue.
Ar-my and Na-vy for-ev-er, Three cheers for the red, white, and blue!

The Blue Bells of Scotland.

Moderato

Scotch.

mf

1. Oh! where, and oh! where is your High-land lad-die gone? Oh! where, and oh!
2. Oh! where, and oh! where did your High-land lad-die dwell? Oh! where, and oh!
3. Sup-pose and sup-pose that your High-land lad should die. Sup-pose and sup-

where is your High-land lad-die gone? He's gone to fight the French for King
where did your High-land lad-die dwell? He dwelt in mer-ry Scot-land at
pose that your High-land lad should die. The bag-pipes would play o'er him, I'd

George up-on the throne, And it's oh! in my heart I wish him safe at home.
sign of the Blue Bell, And it's oh! in my heart I love my lad-die well.
sit me down and cry, And it's oh! in my heart I hope he may not die.

Sunrise.

Allegretto

Naegeli.

f

1. See, where the ris-ing sun In splen-dor decks the skies; His dai-ly
2. Fair is the face of morn, Why should your eye-lids keep Closed when the

FINE.

course be-gun, Haste and a-rise. Oh! come with me where
night is gone? Wake from your sleep. Oh! who would slum-ber

mf

vio-lets bloom And fill the air with sweet per-fume, And
in his bed When dark-ness from his couch is fled; And

D. C.

where, like dia-monds thro' the skies, Dew-drops spar-kle bright.
when the lark as-cends on high, War-bling songs of joy?

Wandering Song.

German.   German.

Andante sostenuto.
p dolce

1. Breez-es soft I feel re-turn-ing, Her-alds of the dew-y spring.
2. Fare thee well, I now must leave thee, Na-tive home to me so dear.
3. God pro-tect thee now and ev-er; Love u-nite us to the end.

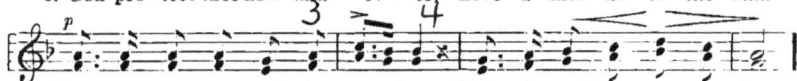

Now my ea-ger soul is yearn-ing; Fain I would be wan-der-ing.
Dis-tant lands wait to re-ceive me; Hope my long-ing heart doth cheer.
Oh! for-get, for-get me nev-er, Think up-on thine ab-sent friend.

Where the white mists hang in shad-ows O'er the mountain peaks and meadows,
Life hath ma-ny a glad be-gin-ning, Ven-tures bold are half the win-ning.
Both, the same bright sun shall glad-den; Let not my de-part-ure sad-den.

Thith-er am I wan-der-ing: Then, my staff oh! quick-ly bring.
Hope the wand'rer's heart doth cheer. Fare thee well, my home so dear.
Think up-on thine ab-sent friend, Love u-nite us to the end.

A Morning Hymn.

Isaac Watts.   W. Volkmann.
Moderato.

1. My God, who makes the sun to know His pro-per hour to
2. When from the cham-ber of the east His morn-ing race be-
3. So, like the sun, would I ful-fill The busi-ness of the

rise, And, to give light to all be-low, Doth
gins, He nev-er tires, nor stops, to rest, But
day; Be-gin my work be-times, and, still, March

send him round the skies, Doth send him round the skies.
round the world he shines, But round the world he shines.
on my heav'n-ly way, March on my heav'n-ly way.

43

Spring, Hurry Along.

Slade. Allegretto. Zelter.

mf

1. Spring, spring, o - 'ver the moun - tains, Why don't you hur - ry a-
2. Birds, birds, far a - way fly - ing, Why don't you hur - ry a-
3. Flow'rs flow'rs, si - lent - ly sleep - ing, Why don't you hur - ry a-
4. Child, child, hear-ing you call - ing, Soon will they hur - ry a-

cresc.

long? I want you to breathe where the white snow-drift lin - gers,
long? I want you to wake me at dawn with your sing - ing,
long? I want to see cro - cus, and snow-drop and lil - y,
long; The spring will soon set all the brook - lets a - flow - ing,

To un - tie the brook with your fin - gers.
I want the air full of notes ring - ing.
And beau - ti - ful daf - fy - down - dil - ly.
The bir - dies a sing - ing the flow'rs a - grow - ing.

mf

Spring, spring, o - ver the moun-tains, Why don't you hur-ry a - long?
Birds, birds, far a - way fly - ing, Why don't you hur-ry a - long?
Flow'rs flow'rs, si - lent - ly sleep - ing, Why don't you hur-ry a - long?
Child, child, hear - ing you call - ing, Soon they will hur-ry a - long.

The Rainbow.

Walter S. Landor. C. A. Kern.

Andante. *dim.*

p

1. I see the rain-bow in the sky, The dew up - on the grass;
2. With fold-ed arms I lin - ger not, To call them back: 'twere vain;

cresc. *dim.*

I see them, and I ask not why They glim-mer or they pass.
In this, or in some oth - er spot I know they'll shine a - gain.

To-day, My Love, To-day.

Charles Mackay.

Allegro.

Mendelssohn.

mf

1. If For-tune, with a smil-ing face, Strew ros-es on our way, When
2. If those who've wrong'd will own their faults, And kind-ly pi-ty pray, When

shall we stoop to pick them up? To-day, my love, to-day. To-day, my love, to-
shall we lis-ten and for-give? To-day, my love, to-day, To-day, my love, to-

p

mf

day. But should she frown, with face of care, And talk of com-ing sor-row,
day. But, if stern just-ice urge re-buke, And warmth from mem'ry bor-row,

p

When shall we grieve, if grieve we must? When shall we grieve, if grieve we must?
When shall we chide, if chide we dare? When shall we chide, if chide we dare?

mf

To-mor-row, love, to-mor-row, To-mor-row, love, to-mor-row.
To-mor-row, love, to-mor-row, To-mor-row, love, to-mor-row.

Immensity of God.

Dulcken.

Moderato.

Fr. Schneider.

mf

f

1. Who can on the sea-shore, Who can on the sea-shore Count the grains of sand?
2. Who can meas-ure o-cean, Who can meas-ure o-cean Where it deep-est flows?
3. God is the un-num-bered, God is the un-num-bered, Who no bounds can know;
4. God is called the bound-less, God is called the bound-less, Fath-om-less is He;

mf

dim.

Or the leaves in au-tumn, Or the leaves in au-tumn, Whirl-ing o'er the land?
Or the rays the sun darts, Or the rays the sun darts When it bright-est glows?
Suns and stars be-fore Him, Suns and stars be-fore Him Are as flakes of snow.
Swift-er than the light-nings, Swift-er then the light-nings, Deep-er than the sea.

Nutting Song.

Emily Huntington Miller.   Arranged from Albert Voelckerling.

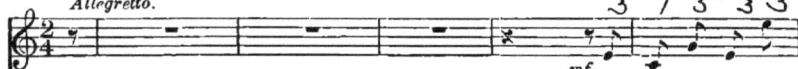

Allegretto.

1. Who has no sun-shine
2. The yel-low moon is
3. Hur - rah! the nuts are

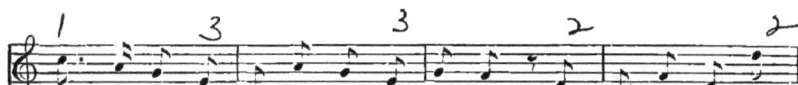

in   his heart May call the au - tumn so - ber;   But boys, with puls - es
clear and bright, The si - lent up - land light-ing;   The mead - ow grass is
drop-ping ripe In   all the wild wood bow - ers;   We'll climb   as high as

leap - ing wild, Should love the brown Oc - to - ber.   A - long   the lake and
crisp and white, The frosts are keen and bit - ing;   A   shin - ing moon, a
squir-rels go, We'll shake them down in show - ers.   When heads   are gray and

on the hill, The rud - dy oaks are glow - ing, And mer - ry winds are
frost - y sky, A gust - y morn to fol - low,—To drive the with - ered
eyes are dim, We'll call the au-tumn so - ber; But now, with life in

out by night, Thro' all the for - ests blow - ing, Thro' all the for - ests
leaves a - bout, And heap them in the hol - low, And heap them in the
ev - 'ry limb, We love the brown Oc - to - ber, We love the brown Oc-

blow-ing, And mer - ry winds are out by night, Thro' all the for-ests blowing.
hol - low, To drive the with-ered leaves a - bout, And heap them in the hol-low.
to - ber, But now, with life in ev - 'ry limb, We love the brown Oc-to-ber.

48   Hail Columbia!

Hopkinson.   *Alla marcia.*   Phyla.

1. Hail! Co-lum-bia, hap-py land, Hail! ye he-roes,
2. Im-mor-tal pa-triots, rise once more, De-fend your rights, de-
3. Sound, sound the trump of fame; Let our own Wash-ing-
4. Be-hold! the chief who now com-mands, Once more, to serve his

heav'n-born band, Who fought and bled in free-dom's cause, Who fought and bled in
fend your shore, Let no rude foe with im-pious hands, Let no rude foe with
ton's great name Ring thro' the world with loud applause, Ring thro' the world with
coun-try, stands, The rock on which the storm will beat, The rock on which the

free-dom's cause, And, when the storm of war was gone, En-joy'd the peace your
im-pious hands In-vade the shrine where sa-cred lies Of toil and blood the
loud ap-plause; Let ev-'ry clime, to free-dom dear, Lis-ten with a
storm will beat, But, sound in vir-tue, firm and true, His hopes are fix'd on

va-lor won. Let in-de-pen-dence be our boast, Ev-er mind-ful
well-earn'd prize. While off-'ring peace sin-cere and just, In heav'n we place a
joy-ful ear. With e-qual skill, with God-like pow'r He gov-erns in the
heav'n and you. When hope was sin-king in dis-may, When glooms obscur'd Co-

what it cost, Ev-er grate-ful for the prize; Let its al-tar
man-ly trust, That truth and jus-tice will pre-vail, And ev-'ry scheme of
hon-est peace. Firm, u-nit-ed let us be, Rally-ing round our lib-er-ty,
lum-bia's day, His stead-y mind, from chan-ges free, Re-solv'd on death or

reach the skies. Firm, u-nit-ed let us be, Rally-ing round our lib-er-ty,
bon-dage fail. Firm, u-nit-ed let us be, Rally-ing round our lib-er-ty,
hon-est peace. Firm, u-nit-ed let us be, Rally-ing round our lib-er-ty,
lib-er-ty, Firm, u-nit-ed let us be, Rally-ing round our lib-er-ty,

As a band of broth-ers join'd, Peace and safe-ty we shall find.

Birds of Passage.

Hoffmann von Fallersleben.

Graben-Hoffmann.

Lento. dolce

1. Oh! field and wood were passing fair; To - day, a - las! the world is bare, The
2. No care we know, but joy and ease; Our roof the tent - ing for - est trees; We
3. But now our homes are roof-less quite, The summer yields to win-ter's night, And

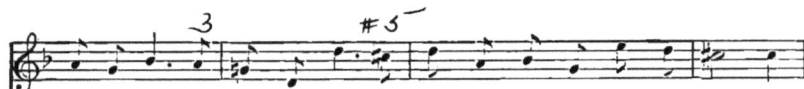

Lento.

p dolce

sum-mer's gone from hill and plain, And aft - er glad-ness fol - lows pain, And
sang a - way the hap - py spring, The wood-land loved to hear us sing, The
we poor, joy-less pil-grim band Must seek a home in stran-ger land, Must

rall.

aft - er gladness follows pain.
wood-land loved to hear us sing.
seek a home in stranger land. *a tempo*

rall.

50

As the Golden Stars of Heaven.

Andantino. German.

1. As the gold-en stars of heav-en Love their az-ure home a-bove,
2. As the rain-bow shines re-flect-ed In the glass-y lake be-low,

p As the ros-y light of e-ven Greets the wea-ry world in love,
As the moon-light is de-tect-ed Shin-ing in the streamlet's glow,

mf As the foun-tains bless the flow-er, As the sun-light loves the bow-er;
As the pur-ple clouds give warning Of the sun be-fore the dawning;

p So all things of good that be, Look, dear Fa-ther, un-to Thee.
So all things of good that be, Are, dear Fa-ther, all from Thee.

Ring, Merry Bells.

Allegro. German.

1. Ring, ring, ring, mer-ry bells, And hail the glad new year; For the
2. Ring, ring, ring, mer-ry bells, And, old year, fare thee well; For of
3. Ring, ring, ring, mer-ry bells, All hail, new year, to thee! May thy

old year's gone, his work is done, And the young and bright new
griefs and fears and toils and tears All thy days and nights were
days and nights bring pure de-lights, And our lives and works much

year is here: Then, wel-come him with ring-ing and sing-ing.
quite too full: We part with thee both sad-ly and glad-ly.
no-bler be, And bring to us full meas-ure of pleas-ure.

A May Song.

Mendelssohn. 51

Alla marcia.

1. All the buds and bees are sing - ing, All the lil - y bells are ring - ing, All the brooks run full of laugh - ter, And the winds come whisp'-ring aft - er. What is this, what is this, what is this they sing and say? It is May, it is May, it is May, it is May. What is this, what is this they sing and say? It is May, it is May, they sing and say.

2. See! the fair, blue sky is bright-er, And our hearts with hope are light - er; All the bells of joy are ring - ing; All the grate - ful voic - es sing - ing; All the storms, all the storms, all the storms have passed a - way. It is May, it is May, it is May, it is May. All the storms, all the storms have passed a - way. It is May, it is May, it is beauti - ful May.

52   The Seasons.

Foxwell.
Andante.   Strum.

1. O bloom-ing spring, O bloom-ing spring, With all my heart I love thee! For
2. O sum - mer time, O sum - mer time, With all my heart I love thee! For
3. O au - tumn brown, O au - tumn brown, With all my heart I love thee! For
4. O win - ter old, O win - ter old, With all my heart I love thee! For

Andante.

per - fume sweet and col - ors gay And ver - dure fresh, shall deck the May, For
wav - ing corn sa-lutes the breeze, And lus - cious fruit adorns the trees, For
var - ied tints will clothe the wood, And plen - ty yield its store of good, For
spar - kling snow and sport - ive ice And Christmas cheer, the tho'ts en-tice, For

perfume sweet and colors gay And ver - dure fresh, shall deck the May.
waving corn salutes the breeze, And lus-cious fruit a - dorns the trees.
varied tints will clothe the wood, And plenty yield its store of good.
sparkling snow and sportive ice And Christmas cheer, the tho'ts en - tice.

New Year Song.

Emily Huntington Miller.

Adapted from R. Mueller.

Allegro moderato.

1. They say that the year is old and gray, That his
2. He brings us a gift from the beau - ti-ful land We

Allegro moderato.

eyes are dim with sor - - row; But
see in our ros - y dream - ing, Where the

what care we, though he pass a - way? For the
won - der-ful cas - tles of fan - cy stand In

New Year Song.

New Year comes to - mor - - row. No
mag - i - cal sun - shine gleam - - ing. Then,

sigh have we for the ros - - es fied, No
sing, young hearts, that are full of cheer, With

tears for the van - ished sum - - mer; Fresh
nev - er a thought of sor - - row; The

New Year Song.

55

flow'rs will spring where the old are dead, To
old goes out, but the glad young year Comes

wel - come the glad new - com - - er.
mer - ri - ly in to - mor - - row.

Robin's Come.

W. W. Caldwell.

Andante.

German.

mf

1. From the elm-tree's top-most bough Hark! the rob-in's ear-ly song,
2. Of the win-ter we are wea-ry, Wea-ry of its frost and snow,
3. Ring it out o'er hill and plain, Through the gar-den's lone-ly bowers,

Tell-ing one and all, that now Mer-ry spring-time hastes a - long;
Long-ing for the sun - shine cheer-y, And the brook-let's gur-gling flow;
Till the green leaves dance a - gain, Till the air is sweet with flowers;

p   *mf*

Tra la, la, la, la, la, la, la, la, la, la; Tra, la, la, la, la, la, la, la, la, la,

f

la; Wel-come, wel-come thou dost bring, Lit-tle har - bin-ger of spring.
la; Glad-ly, then, we hear thee sing The a - wak - en - ing of spring.
la; Make the cow-slip by the rill, Make the yel - low daf - fo - dil.

My Country, 'Tis of Thee.

Moderato.

Carey.

mf

1. My coun - try, 'tis of thee, Sweet land of lib - er - ty,
2. My na - tive coun - try, thee, Land of the no - ble free,
3. Let mu - sic swell the breeze, And ring from all the trees
4. Our fa - thers' God, to Thee, Au - thor of lib - er - ty,

f

Of thee I sing. Land where my fa - thers died, Land of the
Thy name I love; I love thy rocks and rills, Thy woods and
Sweet free - dom's song; Let mor - tal tongues a - wake, Let all that
To Thee we sing. Long may our land be bright With free - dom's

pil-grim's pride; From ev - 'ry moun-tain side Let free - dom ring.
tem - pl'd hills; My heart with rap-ture thrills Like that a - bove.
breathe par - take, Let rocks their si - lence break, The sound pro - long.
ho - ly light, Pro - tect us by Thy might, Great God, our King.

Good Night.

57

German.

Lento. dolce

1. Good night, good night, and peace be with you, Peace, that gen-tlest
2. Good night, good night, but not for ev-er; Hope can see the
3. Good night, good night, oh! soft-ly breathe it, 'Tis a pray'r for

part-ing strain. Soft it falls like dew on blos-soms, Cher-ish-
morn-ing rise, Ma-ny pleas-ant scenes be-fore us, As if
those we love; Peace to-night, and joy to-mor-row, For our

ing with-in our bos-oms Kind de-sires to meet a-gain.
an-gels hov-ered o'er us, Bear-ing bless-ings from the skies.
God, who shields the spar-row, Hears us in His courts a-bove.

Longing.

Caldwell.
Andante.

Hamma.

1. Tell me what the brook doth sing, Wea-ry, wait-ing for the spring?
2. Tell me what does rose-bud sigh, Long-ing for the sum-mer nigh?

cresc.

mf

"Let me free," the brook-let sing-eth, "Win-ter, let me haste a-way."
"Let me blos-som," rose-bud sigh-eth, "Let me o-pen to the day."

Win-ter, stay a-while thy play-ing, Soon the south winds will be blow-ing,
Rose-bud, wait till June comes to you, Then its zeph-yrs soft shall sue you,

pp più lento

And, to set the wind-mills go-ing, You shall haste a-way, a-way.
And its ar-dent sun shall woo you O-pen, o-pen to the day.

Copyright, 1897, by Scott, Foresman & Company.

58

Bells at Eve.

Abt.

Andante con moto.

1. Sweet to hear the bells of eve - ning As a-
2. Sweet to hear the bells of eve - ning As a-
3. Sweet to hear the bells of eve - ning Mingle

cross the flow-'ry lea, Borne up - on the scent-ed zeph-yrs, Comes their
mid the war-blers' song Comes their mu-sic with the ves - pers Car-ol'd
with the brooklet's flow, Join-ing with their sil-v'ry voi - ces In the

dul-cet mel - o - dy! Hearts that may be fill'd with sor-row Own its
by the feath-er'd throng! Hearts that may be fill'd with sor-row Own their
mu-sic soft and low! Hearts that may be fill'd with sor-row Own its

gen-tle, sooth - ing pow'r,   Feel their press-ing bur - den light-en'd   'Neath the
gen-tle, sooth - ing pow'r,   Feel their press-ing bur - den light-en'd   'Neath the
gen-tle, sooth - ing pow'r,   Feel their press-ing bur - den light-en'd   'Neath tho

ma - gic   of   the hour.
ma - gic   of   the hour.
ma - gic   of   the hour.

Ring

p

mf

Più tranquillo.

cresc

on, sweet bells of e - ven,   Ring on, ring on,   ring on,......   Ring

Più tranquillo.

p

Bells at Eve.

on, sweet bells of e - ven, Ring on, ring on, ring on!.......

Begone! Dull Care.

Allegretto.

Old English air, 17th Century.

Be - gone! dull care,.... I pri-thee, be - gone from me.... Be-

gone! dull care, You and I shall nev - er a - gree.... Long

time hast thou been tarry - ing here, And fain thou wouldst me kill.. But i'

faith, dull care,.... Thou nev - er shall have thy will....

October's Bright, Blue Weather.

Helen Hunt Jackson.
By per. of Roberts Bros.

Gruenberger.

Allegretto

1. O suns and skies and clouds of June, And flow'rs of June, to-geth - er Yo
2. When all the love-ly way-side things Their white-winged seeds are sowing, And

can - not ri - val for one hour Oc - to-ber's bright, blue weath-er! When
in the fields, still green and fair, Late aft - er-maths are grow-ing. O

cresc.

on the ground red ap - ples lie In piles, like jew - els shin - ing, And
suns and skies and flow'rs of June! Count all your boasts to - geth - er; Love

mf *cresc.*

red - der still on old stone walls Are leaves of wood-bine twin-ing.
lov - eth best of all the year Oc - to-ber's bright, blue weath-er.

Chorus. *a tempo*

f

O suns and skies and clouds of June, And flow'rs of June, to-geth - er Yo

can - not ri - val for one hour Oc - to-ber's bright, blue weath-er!

Oh! How Pleasant is the Evening.
ROUND.

Andante.
p dolce

O. Schulz.

Oh! how pleas-ant is the even-ing, is the even-ing, When the bells are

sweet - ly ring - ing, sweet-ly ring - ing; Bim, bom, bim, bom, bim, bom!

The North Wind Doth Blow.

C. A. Kern.

Allegro. cresc

mf

1. The north-wind doth blow, and we shall have snow, And
2. The north-wind doth blow, and we shall have snow, And
3. The north-wind doth blow, and we shall have snow, And

dim   *dim.*   *p*

what will poor rob-in do then? poor thing! And what will poor rob-in do
what will the bee do then? poor thing! And what will the bee do
what will the children do then? poor things! And what will the children do

mf   *cresc.*

then? poor thing! He'll sit in the barn, and
then? poor thing! In his hive he will stay till the
then? poor things! When les-sons are done they'll

f

keep him-self warm, And hide his head un-der his wing, poor thing!
cold's passed a-way, And then he'll come out in the spring, poor thing!
jump, skip, and run, And that's how they'll keep themselves warm, poor things!

The Lorelei.

Heine. Andante.

Silcher.

1. I know not what comes o'er me That thus my spir - its fail, Strange
2. A strange-ly beau - teous maid - en Up yon - der I be - hold, With
3. The boat-man sits and gaz - es, He feels a com - ing woe, His

vis-ions a - rise be - fore me, I think of an an - cient tale. The
trin-kets of gold she's lad - en, She han-dles a comb of gold. While
eye to the height he rais - es, But sees not the rocks be - low. The

air is cool, and 'tis dark-ling While gen-tly flows the Rhine; The
comb-ing her gold - en tress - es, She sings a won-drous song; The
Lor - e - lei's song he must fol-low; I know what she will do, The

tops of the moun-tains are spar-kling, In the ev' - ning red they shine.
hear - er's soul she pos - ses - ses, And hur - ries it a - long.
bil-lows too soon will swal - low The boat and boat-man too.

INDEX

www.ingramcontent.com/pod-product-compliance
Lightning Source LLC
Chambersburg PA
CBHW021530090426
42739CB00007B/859